This book belongs to

....

HOW TO USE THIS BOOK

Congratulations, you're getting married! Now is the time to get organised and thereby minimise the stress of planning your wedding. Even a relatively small wedding takes a degree of organisation – ringing round asking for quotes, choosing this option over that – if you are not well organised it can be tricky remembering what you've agreed to or why one quote was cheaper than another. Worse than that, it can be easy to miss payment deadlines and run the risk of bookings being cancelled.

The Wedding Planner has been designed so you can keep everything in one place. It's small enough to carry round with you and has a pocket to keep clippings, business cards and notes to hand. Use the year planners to keep a sense of the whole picture, and then the month by month planners for specific appointments. The fourteen sections cover all aspects of planning your wedding from budgeting to booking your honeymoon.

Every wedding is different and so it is never going to be a question of 'one size fits all'. Where we have given suggestions they are just that, and we have left blank spaces throughout for you to fill in your own options. As well as being a useful planning tool, we hope the planner can give you space to be creative, and help you track your progress from ideas and inspiration to your dream wedding day. Have fun!

PLANNING

Use the following list as a memory jogger to tick off when things are completed. Not everything may be relevant for what you have planned and, of course, the timings are only guidelines. But remember, popular venues and suppliers do get booked up quickly so try and plan well in advance. We've left some blank spaces for you to add anything specific you may want to remember, and there are also the monthly and weekly diary sheets you can use to make notes of appointments and things to do.

AFTER YOU GET ENGAGED

- Tell relatives and friends
- Plan an engagement party
- Agree a budget and decide who is paying for what
- If you are having a religious ceremony, organise a meeting with the cleric to arrange and book the date
- If you are having a civil ceremony, book the venue or register office
- Make an initial guest list to get an idea of numbers
- Choose your attendants (bridesmaids/men, best man/woman, ushers etc)
- Visit possible venues for the reception
- Discuss menu options and get quotes for food and drink
- Confirm reception venue as soon as you can
- Start gathering ideas for your wedding outfit and your attendants' outfits
- Get quotes and book your photographer and videographer
- Organise wedding insurance
- _____
- _____

3–6 MONTHS BEFORE YOUR WEDDING

- Make sure your friends and family know the date so everyone keeps it free
- Arrange to see the person officiating at the ceremony so you can discuss the order of service
- Organise the marriage licence
- Choose readings, hymns and music for the ceremony
- Ask friends or family to do the readings
- Organise a choir, organist etc as appropriate
- Organise music for the reception as required
- Choose and order the wedding cake
- Choose your florist and discuss your plans
- Arrange any wedding outfit fittings
- Look for accessories for you and your attendants

- ○ Book hotels and transport for your first night and honeymoon as necessary
- ○ Discuss hairstyles with your hairdresser/barber
- ○ Check passports are valid and organise vaccinations and/or visas if appropriate
- ○ Choose your wedding rings
- ○ Book wedding cars and any other transport required
- ○ Set up your gift list
- ○ Buy gifts for the attendants
- ○ Choose and order your stationery
- ○ _____
- ○ _____

2 MONTHS BEFORE YOUR WEDDING
- ○ Book hair and make-up appointments for the day
- ○ Finalise the order of service
- ○ Reconfirm all bookings in writing
- ○ Order any favours or table decorations
- ○ Send out invitations with gift list details if required
- ○ Send out thank you notes as gifts arrive
- ○ Check all outfits are organised
- ○ Finalise the menu
- ○ _____
- ○ _____

1 MONTH BEFORE YOUR WEDDING
- ○ If you are changing your name, inform your bank and other institutions
- ○ Confirm all reception details and the timetable in writing
- ○ _____
- ○ _____

2 WEEKS BEFORE YOUR WEDDING
- ○ Try on your full wedding outfit and make sure you feel comfortable
- ○ Confirm final numbers and prepare the seating plan
- ○ Start packing for your honeymoon
- ○ Confirm all hair and make-up appointments
- ○ Confirm all pick-up times and addresses with your transport provider
- ○ Organise airport and station pick-ups for any family/friends arriving from abroad or long distance

WEDDING COUNTDOWN

- ○ Arrange a wedding rehearsal date for the week before the big day
- ○ Write vows if appropriate
- ○ _____
- ○ _____

I WEEK BEFORE YOUR WEDDING

- ○ Make sure the florist, photographer and videographer are briefed
- ○ Arrange for delivery of all favours and table decorations to the venue
- ○ Plan in some time for relaxing!
- ○ Distribute wedding day contact details and make sure everyone knows what is required of them
- ○ Attend the wedding rehearsal
- ○ _____
- ○ _____

THE DAY BEFORE YOUR WEDDING

- ○ Decorate the venue with the help of friends and family if necessary
- ○ Arrange for the cake to be delivered to the venue
- ○ Gather together everything you will need for the day
- ○ _____
- ○ _____

THE BIG DAY

- ○ Make sure you leave yourself plenty of time to get ready
- ○ Have a good breakfast
- ○ Have buttonholes and other flowers delivered or collected
- ○ _____
- ○ _____

AFTER YOUR WEDDING

- ○ Return any hired items and collect deposits
- ○ Consider preserving your bouquet/other flowers
- ○ Finish off sending thank you cards
- ○ Arrange delivery of your gifts
- ○ Collect your wedding photos and video
- ○ Dry-clean your wedding outfits
- ○ _____
- ○ _____

JANUARY	JULY
FEBRUARY	AUGUST
MARCH	SEPTEMBER
APRIL	OCTOBER
MAY	NOVEMBER
JUNE	DECEMBER

JANUARY	JULY
FEBRUARY	AUGUST
MARCH	SEPTEMBER
APRIL	OCTOBER
MAY	NOVEMBER
JUNE	DECEMBER

MONTH:

1
2
3
4
5
6
7
8
9
10
11
12
13
14
15
16
17
18
19
20
21
22
23
24
25
26
27
28
29
30
31

MONTH:

1
2
3
4
5
6
7
8
9
10
11
12
13
14
15
16
17
18
19
20
21
22
23
24
25
26
27
28
29
30
31

MONTH:

1
2
3
4
5
6
7
8
9
10
11
12
13
14
15
16
17
18
19
20
21
22
23
24
25
26
27
28
29
30
31

MONTH:

1
2
3
4
5
6
7
8
9
10
11
12
13
14
15
16
17
18
19
20
21
22
23
24
25
26
27
28
29
30
31

1
2
3
4
5
6
7
8
9
10
11
12
13
14
15
16
17
18
19
20
21
22
23
24
25
26
27
28
29
30
31

MONTH:

1
2
3
4
5
6
7
8
9
10
11
12
13
14
15
16
17
18
19
20
21
22
23
24
25
26
27
28
29
30
31

1
2
3
4
5
6
7
8
9
10
11
12
13
14
15
16
17
18
19
20
21
22
23
24
25
26
27
28
29
30
31

MONTH:

1
2
3
4
5
6
7
8
9
10
11
12
13
14
15
16
17
18
19
20
21
22
23
24
25
26
27
28
29
30
31

1
2
3
4
5
6
7
8
9
10
11
12
13
14
15
16
17
18
19
20
21
22
23
24
25
26
27
28
29
30
31

MONTH:

1
2
3
4
5
6
7
8
9
10
11
12
13
14
15
16
17
18
19
20
21
22
23
24
25
26
27
28
29
30
31

MONTH:

1
2
3
4
5
6
7
8
9
10
11
12
13
14
15
16
17
18
19
20
21
22
23
24
25
26
27
28
29
30
31

1
2
3
4
5
6
7
8
9
10
11
12
13
14
15
16
17
18
19
20
21
22
23
24
25
26
27
28
29
30
31

WEEKLY PLANNER

MONDAY

TUESDAY

WEDNESDAY

THURSDAY

FRIDAY

SATURDAY

SUNDAY

WEEKLY PLANNER

MONDAY

TUESDAY

WEDNESDAY

THURSDAY

FRIDAY

SATURDAY

SUNDAY

WEEKLY PLANNER

MONDAY

TUESDAY

WEDNESDAY

THURSDAY

FRIDAY

SATURDAY

SUNDAY

WEDDING DAY TIMETABLE

The following is a guide to the order in which events might unfold on the day. You may choose not to include all these or you may have other appointments you want to plan for. It's important that key players know what is supposed to be happening and when, as this will take the strain off of you and your partner. Use this sheet to plan what works for your day and then create your own personalized timetable on the following page, photocopy and distribute as necessary. You may want to do one for you and one for your fiancé, as they might be slightly different in the early stages of the day.

GET UP

BREAKFAST

BUTTONHOLES/CORSAGES DELIVERED

GROOM AND BEST MAN LEAVE FOR CEREMONY

BRIDE AND BRIDESMAIDS LEAVE FOR CEREMONY

USHERS ARRIVE AT CEREMONY

PHOTOS BEFORE THE CEREMONY

GUESTS ARRIVE

WEDDING CEREMONY BEGINS

FORMAL WEDDING PHOTOGRAPHS

LEAVE FOR THE RECEPTION

ARRIVE AT THE RECEPTION

MEAL TO BE SERVED

TOASTS & SPEECHES

CAKE CUTTING

FIRST DANCE

BRIDE & GROOM CHANGE CLOTHES

BRIDE & GROOM LEAVE RECEPTION

RECEPTION ENDS

BRIDE	GROOM
PHONE:	PHONE:
ATTENDANTS:	ATTENDANTS:
PHONE:	PHONE:
PHONE:	PHONE:
PHONE:	PHONE:
PHONE:	PHONE:
PHONE:	PHONE:
PHONE:	PHONE:
PHONE:	PHONE:

MOTHER OF THE BRIDE

PHONE:

FATHER OF THE BRIDE

PHONE:

TRANSPORT

PHONE:

CEREMONY VENUE

PHONE:

EVENING VENUE

PHONE:

REGISTRAR

PHONE:

CATERER

PHONE:

PHOTOGRAPHER

PHONE:

FLORIST

PHONE:

MOTHER OF THE GROOM

PHONE:

FATHER OF THE GROOM

PHONE:

DJ/BAND

PHONE:

EMERGENCY TAXIS

PHONE:

OTHER:

PHONE:

PHONE:

PHONE:

PHONE:

PHONE:

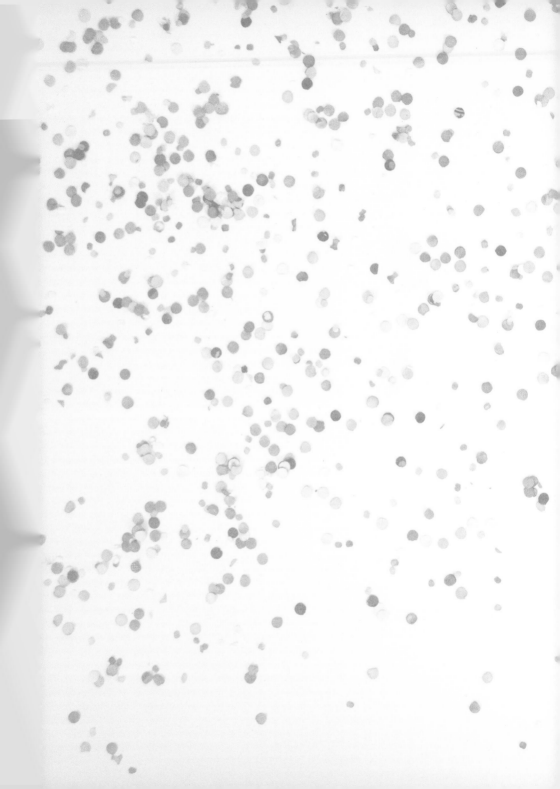

INSPIRATION

INSPIRATION / NOTES

Use the following pages to collect your sources of inspiration. Clip or paste in pictures from magazines, add swatches of colour, or jot down website recommendations, favourite social media accounts, and magazines to buy or subscribe to. Use the moodboards to allow you to visualise different themes and ideas – get creative!

space to collect your ideas

space to collect your ideas

BUDGET

BUDGET CHECKLIST

○   Set your budget as soon as possible and keep checking to make sure you are on track. Then if you overspend in one area, perhaps you can make savings in another.

○   Take the time early on to discuss what is most important to you both and prioritise the rest – it will make decisions much easier further down the line.

○   Discuss as early as possible who is expecting to pay for what so there are no surprises. Nowadays many couples pay for the lion's share of their wedding costs.

○   Avoid over-using the credit card – it would be a shame to start married life in debt.

○   Work out roughly how much you think *every* item will cost you – it is often the little things that you forget and these add up quickly.

○   Read magazines and get advice from them but beware, it is easy to succumb to wedding fever and find yourself committing to things you never would have dreamed of. Every so often do a reality check to find out if you really need that extra detail.

○   There are plenty of ways to save money – make use of family and friends' talent whether it's for baking cakes, music, arranging flowers or perhaps someone owns a vintage car that can get you to the church on time.

○   If you want to save money, consider holding your wedding out of season and you may get some good deals from specialist services.

○   Choosing seasonal food and flowers will often mean better value and better quality. Try to source locally too, if possible.

○   Make sure you get detailed written quotations for everything and pay your deposits on time to avoid penalities or cancellation.

○   Check whether VAT or sales tax is included in the quotations or if it will be added on top.

○   Always ask if there are any other charges you need to know about – there can be differences between suppliers about what services are included or not.

○ Remember that gratuities are often expected and not always included in the quotations (but they may be).

○ You will need to pay for some things on the day so find out whether you need cash or can use a credit card and who is going to be responsible for doing what. Organise as much in advance as possible and delegate, delegate, delegate!

○ If you are offering a 'free bar' on the night, ask a trusted friend or relative (preferably one who won't be drinking) to be responsible for checking the ongoing tally and signing off the bills at agreed stages through the evening.

○ Remember to check what bills may come in while you are away on honeymoon and work out how you're going to pay them or have the payment date moved.

○ Don't be afraid to negotiate or ask for deals where possible. Sometimes you can get a discount or a service for free if others in the bridal party are using the same facility.

....

notes

WEDDING BUDGET

ITEM	BUDGETED COST
ENGAGEMENT RINGS	
BRIDE'S WEDDING RING	
GROOM'S WEDDING RING	
BRIDE'S ATTIRE	
GROOM'S ATTIRE	
BRIDE'S BEAUTY/HAIRCARE	
GROOM'S BARBER	
WEDDING CARS/TRANSPORT	
PHOTOGRAPHY	
RECEPTION VENUE	
CATERING	
DRINKS	
WEDDING CAKE	
FAVOURS	
ENTERTAINMENT	
THANK YOU GIFTS	
FIRST-NIGHT HOTEL	
HONEYMOON	
TOTAL	

REVISED BUDGET	ACTUAL COST

INDIVIDUAL BUDGET FOR:

DETAILS	SUPPLIER	QUOTE

BUDGETED COST	ACTUAL COST
TOTAL CARRIED FORWARD TO WEDDING BUDGET SUMMARY:	

INDIVIDUAL BUDGET FOR:

DETAILS	SUPPLIER	QUOTE

BUDGETED COST	ACTUAL COST
TOTAL CARRIED FORWARD TO WEDDING BUDGET SUMMARY:	

PAYMENTS DUE AT-A-GLANCE

SUPPLIER NAME & CONTACT DETAILS	SERVICE	CONTRACT DATE & TOTAL
		....
		....
		....
		....
		....
		....
		....
		....

DEPOSIT AMOUNT, DATE DUE & DATE PAID	FINAL PAYMENT AMOUNT, DATE DUE & DATE PAID
JE: PAID:	DUE: PAID:
JE: PAID:	DUE: PAID:
JE: PAID:	DUE: PAID:
JE: PAID:	DUE: PAID:
JE: PAID:	DUE: PAID:
JE: PAID:	DUE: PAID:
JE: PAID:	DUE: PAID:
JE: PAID:	DUE: PAID:
JE: PAID:	DUE: PAID:

CEREMONY

○   Check online for the legal requirements for getting married. www.gro.gov.uk
    (England and Wales), www.gro-scotland.gov.uk (Scotland), www.groireland.ie
    (Ireland).

○   Check online for the religious requirements for getting married. (In the UK at
    www.cofe.anglican.org for the Church of England, www.churchofscotland.org.uk
    for the Church of Scotland, www.catholic-ew.org.uk for the Catholic Church, or
    with the relevant religious organisation.)

○   Researching your ceremony venue is a priority. Popular places get booked up
    months in advance.

○   Try and get some personal recommendations and recent feedback on your
    chosen venue. What the venue boasts on their website may not reflect the reality
    of their service.

○   If you are opting for a civil ceremony, make sure your venue is properly licensed.
    They should be able to give you the relevant contacts for the registrar.

○   If you are opting for a religious service talk to the officiator and explore your
    options – particularly if different faiths are involved. It may be possible to
    combine different elements to create a ceremony unique to you.

○   Explore what restrictions, if any, are tied to the venue (see Questions to
    Ask When Comparing Venues overleaf) particularly with regard to filming,
    photography and confetti.

○   Discuss timings and music, readings and the order of service with the officiator if
    possible as they can usually offer good advice.

○   Find out if you can write you own vows and/or personalize the service in any way.

○   If your ceremony and reception venue are different consider the distance
    between them. Ideally you would not want to travel more than 30 minutes
    between the two.

○   Consider how guests will travel from the ceremony to the reception (see
    Transport), and what parking is available for them. It may be sensible to arrange
    group transport.

○   Discuss what fees are involved and when they should be paid.

○   Decide in advance who will be your witnesses.

○   Find out if any other weddings are planned on the same day. Perhaps you could share the costs for flowers.

○   Find out what leeway there is (if at all) if you are running late.

....

notes

Not all the questions below may be relevant for you — and you may have other questions too that you want to ask. Think about what is important to you and make a note of all your questions beforehand so you can ask them all in one visit or phone call. Make notes on the Comparing sheets so you can compare later.

WHAT DATES ARE AVAILABLE?

WHAT TIMES ARE AVAILABLE?

WHAT IS THE DENOMINATION, IF ANY?

HOW MUCH WILL IT COST?

WHEN WILL THE FEE HAVE TO BE PAID? (WHEN IS THE DEPOSIT DUE?)

WHAT IS YOUR CANCELLATION POLICY?

DOES THE FACILITY HAVE LIABILITY INSURANCE?

WHAT IS THE MINIMUM & MAXIMUM NUMBER OF GUESTS ALLOWED?

WHAT RESTRICTIONS ARE THERE WITH REGARDS TO RELIGION, IF ANY?

IS AN OFFICIATOR AVAILABLE? IF SO, AT WHAT COST?

ARE OUTSIDE OFFICIATORS ALLOWED?

WHAT MUSIC IS AVAILABLE ON SITE & AT WHAT COST?

IS THERE A CHOIR AVAILABLE AND IF SO, AT WHAT COST?

WHAT RESTRICTIONS ON MUSIC ARE THERE, IF ANY?

WHAT PHOTOGRAPHY/FILMING RESTRICTIONS ARE THERE, IF ANY?

WHAT POLICY IS THERE ON CONFETTI?

WHAT POLICY IS THERE WITH REGARD TO CANDLES/NAKED FLAMES?

ARE ANY FLORAL DECORATIONS AVAILABLE, AND IF SO AT WHAT COST?

WHEN CAN A REHEARSAL BE SCHEDULED?

IS THERE DISABLED ACCESS & PARKING?

WHAT PARKING IS AVAILABLE FOR GUESTS?

WHAT PUBLIC TRANSPORT IS AVAILABLE FOR GUESTS?

WILL ANY OTHER CEREMONIES BE SCHEDULED ON THE SAME DAY?

COMPARING

NAME:

ADDRESS:

WEBSITE:
EMAIL:
PHONE:

NAME:

ADDRESS:

WEBSITE:
EMAIL:
PHONE:

COMPARING

NAME: ADDRESS: WEBSITE: EMAIL: PHONE:	NAME: ADDRESS: WEBSITE: EMAIL: PHONE:

COMPARING

NAME: ADDRESS: WEBSITE: EMAIL: PHONE:	NAME: ADDRESS: WEBSITE: EMAIL: PHONE:

COMPARING

NAME:	NAME:
ADDRESS:	ADDRESS:
WEBSITE:	WEBSITE:
EMAIL:	EMAIL:
PHONE:	PHONE:

CEREMONY SUMMARY

VENUE: ....

ADDRESS: ....

....

WEBSITE: ....

CONTACT NAME: ....

PHONE: ....

EMAIL: ....

CEREMONY DATE: _____ TIME: _____

ACCESS FOR FLOWERS FROM: _____ TIME: _____

VENUE TO BE CLEARED BY: _____ TIME: _____

REHEARSAL DATE: _____ TIME: _____

OFFICIATOR: ....

PHONE: ....

EMAIL: ....

AGREED FEE: ....

WITNESSESES: ....

....

ORGANIST: ....

....

CHOIR: ....

....

....

....

AGREED ORDER OF SERVICE

Discuss your order of service with your officiator if possible. They will often be able to offer useful advice on timings, suggested readings and music.

APPROX. TIME	SERVICE

READINGS SELECTION

Readings can be religious or secular – such as a poem or a piece of prose. Suggestions can be readily found on wedding websites. Your officiator may be able to offer some suggestions too. Make sure your readers are clear about when they are on and how much time they have. Ideally they should be included in any rehearsal if possible.

SUGGESTIONS FOR READINGS:

READING	READ BY	WHEN

MUSIC SELECTION

If you are using a laptop, CDs or other device for your music, make sure someone is delegated to collect them at the end of the ceremony or else make arrangements for someone to pick them up after the event. Don't forget to give the person responsible for the music during the ceremony a clear list of what you want and when.

SUGGESTIONS FOR MUSIC:

MUSIC SELECTION	WHEN	SUPPLIED?

CLOTHING

WHAT TO WEAR CHECKLIST

○ Whether you are having your outfit made, buying off the peg or going for haute couture, try on as many different styles as you can to find out what suits you. Different styles suit different people, and you want to feel comfortable, as well as your most beautiful self.

○ Always take someone with you, whose advice you trust, to get a second opinion.

○ At the same time, don't be pressured by the opinions of the sales assistant or friends and family – you want to wear something that makes *you* feel good.

○ Leave plenty of time – if you're having something made, there could be a very long lead time, and this could still apply to off the peg in some cases.

○ Read wedding magazines, blogs and websites for the latest styles and ideas.

○ When you are trying on dresses, wear, or take along, dress shoes and do your make-up – it makes a difference!

○ If you are having a veil select a length that complements the length of your train.

○ Consider the whole look including shoes and accessories before making a final decision.

○ Some shops offer a free headpiece or veil so check before purchasing a gown.

○ Try on your outfit with the underwear you plan to wear, incase of some unexpected bulkiness/visible straps etc.

○ Find someone in advance who can make alterations if required and compare quotes with those offered by the boutique.

○ Order your outfit to allow enough time for last-minute alterations too. Make sure you try it on a few weeks before in case it needs adjusting.

○ If you are on a budget, consider hiring or buying second-hand or vintage or in the sales.

- If you feel confident (or a have a creative friend), buying a plain gown and embellishing it yourself is a good way to save money as well as creating something unique.

- Consider the time of year and location of the wedding when you are choosing a style – what is suitable for high summer in a romantic castle setting may be very different to a chic city registry office wedding.

- Don't forget about choosing your jewellery but remember less is often best.

- Choose comfortable shoes and wear them in a bit – you will be on your feet all day!

....

notes

THE BRIDE'S OUTFIT CHECKLIST

ITEM	DESCRIPTION/SOURCE	BUDGET	ACTUAL COST

THE BRIDE'S OUTFIT

STORE NAME:

ADDRESS:

WEBSITE:

PHONE:

EMAIL:

DESCRIPTION:

DATE ORDERED: _____

DATE OF FITTING: _____

DATE READY: _____

NOTES:

THE GROOM'S OUTFIT CHECKLIST

ITEM	DESCRIPTION/SOURCE	BUDGET	ACTUAL COST

THE GROOM'S OUTFIT

STORE NAME:

ADDRESS:

WEBSITE:

PHONE:

EMAIL:

DESCRIPTION:

DATE ORDERED: _____

DATE OF FITTING: _____

DATE READY: _____

NOTES:

On these pages you can plan outfit details for bridesmaids, best man, ushers etc. Clarify as soon as possible who is paying for what. Attendants often pay for their own outfits but do be clear about this from the start to avoid embarrassment. It may be worth ordering from one local store to take advantage of any discounts but do try and make sure everyone can have a fitting enough time in advance to allow for adjustments.

NAME	SIZE/MEASUREMENTS

ATTENDANTS' OUTFITS

Here you can list individual items of clothing for your attendant's outfits, and their cost (eg. dress, suit, shoes, jewellery, hairdressing).

ITEM	DESCRIPTION/SOURCE	BUDGET	ACTUAL COST

ATTENDANTS' OUTFITS

ORDER DETAILS:

STORE NAME:

ADDRESS:

PHONE:

EMAIL:

DESCRIPTION:

DATE READY: _____

ORDER DETAILS:

STORE NAME:

ADDRESS:

PHONE:

EMAIL:

DESCRIPTION:

DATE READY: _____

FITTINGS & ALTERATIONS SCHEDULE

NAME	DATE	TIME

BEAUTY

BEAUTY CHECKLIST

O   Read wedding magazines, blogs and websites for the latest styles and ideas.

O   Take along visuals and clippings with ideas about styles and colour schemes to your make-up/hair consultation.

O   Make sure you know whether your consultation is going to be free, and if not how much it will cost (and factor it into your budget).

O   If you're wearing one, take your headpiece along with you when you go to your hairdresser to talk about wedding day styles.

O   If you are not having a professional do your make-up on the day perhaps see if you can get some tips from in-store professionals in advance.

O   Always do a trial run of full make-up before the day so you feel confident about what you are doing and know you have everything you need.

O   If you're getting your make-up done professionally, consider whether you want them to do your attendants too, and discuss it with them.

O   A professional manicure and/or pedicure can be a great finishing touch – take your chosen nail polish colour along with you.

O   You want to feel as relaxed as possible on the day – you could book in a massage or spa day close to the wedding, to make you feel extra rested and glowing.

O   You may want to think about packing a little bag to have somewhere handy on the day, with makeup for touch-ups, a hairbrush, painkillers, safety pins, mints etc.

QUESTIONS TO ASK HAIR STYLIST

ARE YOU AVAILABLE ON MY CHOSEN DATE?

HOW MANY YEARS HAVE YOU BEEN IN BUSINESS?

CAN YOU MAKE SOME SUGGESTIONS IN LINE WITH MY BUDGET?

WHAT ARE YOUR RATES?

WHAT IS YOUR CANCELLATION POLICY?

CAN YOU WORK WITH HEADPIECES/ FLOWERS?

WILL YOU BE ABLE TO STYLE MY ATTENDANTS?

WILL YOU HAVE ANY OTHER APPOINTMENTS BOOKED THAT DAY?

DO YOU HAVE A BACK-UP IF YOU CAN'T MAKE IT ON THE DAY?

DO YOU CHARGE FOR CONSULTATIONS?

CAN YOU SUPPLY REFERENCES?

COMPARING

NAME: ADDRESS: WEBSITE: EMAIL: PHONE:	NAME: ADDRESS: WEBSITE: EMAIL: PHONE:

COMPARING

NAME: ADDRESS: WEBSITE: EMAIL: PHONE:	NAME: ADDRESS: WEBSITE: EMAIL: PHONE:

HAIR STYLIST CONFIRMATION

COMPANY NAME:
ADDRESS:

WEBSITE:
CONTACT NAME:
PHONE:
EMAIL:

DETAILS OF BOOKING:

BOOKING CONFIRMED: _____ (DATE) COST: _____
CONTACT:

DEPOSIT: _____ (DUE) _____ (PAID)
BALANCE: _____ (DUE) _____ (PAID)

ARE YOU AVAILABLE ON MY CHOSEN DATE?

HOW MANY YEARS HAVE YOU BEEN IN BUSINESS?

CAN YOU MAKE SOME SUGGESTIONS IN LINE WITH MY BUDGET?

WHAT ARE YOUR RATES?

WHAT IS YOUR CANCELLATION POLICY?

DO I HAVE TO PROVIDE ANYTHING?

WILL YOU BE ABLE TO STYLE MY ATTENDANTS?

WILL YOU HAVE ANY OTHER APPOINTMENTS BOOKED THAT DAY?

DO YOU HAVE A BACK-UP IF YOU CAN'T MAKE IT ON THE DAY?

DO YOU CHARGE FOR CONSULTATIONS?

CAN YOU SUPPLY REFERENCES?

COMPARING

NAME: ADDRESS: WEBSITE: EMAIL: PHONE:	NAME: ADDRESS: WEBSITE: EMAIL: PHONE:

NAME:	NAME:
ADDRESS:	ADDRESS:
WEBSITE: EMAIL: PHONE:	WEBSITE: EMAIL: PHONE:

MAKE-UP CONFIRMATION

COMPANY NAME:

ADDRESS:

WEBSITE:

CONTACT NAME:

PHONE:

EMAIL:

DETAILS OF BOOKING:

BOOKING CONFIRMED: _____ (DATE) COST: _____

CONTACT:

DEPOSIT: _____ (DUE) _____ (PAID)

BALANCE: _____ (DUE) _____ (PAID)

FLOWERS

BOUQUETS & BUTTONHOLES

○ Fresh flowers contribute so much to a wedding – they can reinforce a theme, a colour scheme and set the style – so take your time in deciding what you would like.

○ Browse through bridal magazines and websites and tear/print out images you dislike, as well as those you like. Showing both options to your florist will help them get a better picture of what you are looking for.

○ Take along sketches, visuals and clippings with ideas about shape, style, themes and colour schemes.

○ It is your wedding so don't let anyone bully you into having something you don't want but likewise listen to your florist. They will have lots of experience and advice to offer.

○ When you visit the florist, take a picture or sketch of your outfit as well as swatches of the fabric with you.

○ Be clear about your budget from the start. You can save money by sticking to flowers that are in season and some styles cost less – for example, hand-tied bouquets are cheaper than something that has to have individually-wired flowers.

○ Remember that it's worth asking the ceremony venue if you can share flowers and their cost with anyone else who is getting married on the same day.

....

notes

you may want the following flowers

- ○ Bride's bouquet
- ○ Chief bridesmaid's bouquet
- ○ Bridesmaids' bouquets
- ○ Bride's hair garland
- ○ Chief bridesmaid's/bridesmaids' hair garland(s)
- ○ Flower girl's hair garland
- ○ Corsages
- ○ Groom's buttonhole
- ○ Best man and ushers' buttonholes
- ○ Other buttonholes
- ○ Ceremony: Main altar/front area
- ○ Ceremony: Altar candelabra/side area
- ○ Ceremony: Aisle seats/pews
- ○ Ceremony: _____
  _____
  _____

- ○ Reception top table: _____
  _____

- ○ Reception tables: _____
  _____

- ○ Reception: _____
  _____
  _____

ARE YOU AVAILABLE ON MY CHOSEN DATE?

HOW MANY YEARS HAVE YOU BEEN IN BUSINESS?

WHAT PERCENTAGE OF YOUR BUSINESS IS WEDDINGS?

WHAT IS THE PAYMENT POLICY?

HOW MUCH WOULD THE DEPOSIT BE AND WHEN IS IT PAYABLE?

WHEN IS THE BALANCE PAYABLE?

WHAT IS YOUR CANCELLATION POLICY?

DO YOU HAVE ANY LIABILITY INSURANCE?

WHAT ARE YOUR DELIVERY AND SET-UP FEES?

WILL YOU OR ANOTHER MEMBER OF YOUR TEAM BE DOING THE FLOWERS?

DO YOU HAVE ACCESS TO OUT-OF-SEASON FLOWERS?

CAN YOU MAKE SOME SUGGESTIONS IN LINE WITH MY BUDGET?

WILL YOU USE ALTERNATIVE FLOWERS IF MY CHOSEN FLOWERS ARE NOT AVAILABLE ON THE DAY?

ARE YOU FAMILIAR WITH MY CHOSEN VENUE?

WILL YOU VISIT MY VENUE TO MAKE RECOMMENDATIONS?

WHAT TIME WILL YOU ARRIVE TO DECORATE THE VENUE?

DO YOU RENT OUT VASES/CANDLEHOLDERS ETC AND IF SO, AT WHAT COST?

CAN YOU PRESERVE MY BOUQUET?

WHAT IS YOUR COST OF A BRIDAL BOUQUET MADE OF A DOZEN _____ ?

WHAT IS YOUR COST FOR A BUTTONHOLE MADE OF A SINGLE _____ ?

WHAT IS YOUR COST FOR A CORSAGE MADE UP OF _____ ?

tip

Asking standard questions such as the last three above will give you a good benchmark to compare prices between suppliers. You can then ask more specific questions about particular flowers later.

COMPARING

NAME: ADDRESS: WEBSITE: EMAIL: PHONE:	NAME: ADDRESS: WEBSITE: EMAIL: PHONE:

COMPARING

NAME: ADDRESS: WEBSITE: EMAIL: PHONE:	NAME: ADDRESS: WEBSITE: EMAIL: PHONE:

FLORIST CONFIRMATION

COMPANY NAME: ....

ADDRESS: ....

....

....

WEBSITE: ....

CONTACT NAME: ....

PHONE: ....

EMAIL: ....

DETAILS OF BOOKING: ....

....

....

....

....

....

....

....

....

....

....

....

....

BOOKING CONFIRMED: _____ (DATE) COST: _____

CONTACT: ....

DEPOSIT: _____ (DUE) _____ (PAID)

BALANCE: _____ (DUE) _____ (PAID)

FLOWER PLANNER

BRIDE'S BOUQUET

STYLE/SHAPE:

COLOUR SCHEME:

FLOWERS:

GREENERY:

OTHER (RIBBONS ETC):

COST:

BOUQUET FOR:

STYLE/SHAPE:

COLOUR SCHEME:

FLOWERS:

GREENERY:

OTHER (RIBBONS ETC):

COST:

FLOWER PLANNER

BOUQUET FOR: _____

STYLE/SHAPE ....

COLOUR SCHEME: ....

FLOWERS: ....

....

....

....

....

....

GREENERY: ....

....

....

OTHER (RIBBONS ETC): ....

COST: ....

BOUQUET FOR: _____

STYLE/SHAPE ....

COLOUR SCHEME: ....

FLOWERS: ....

....

....

....

GREENERY ....

....

....

OTHER (RIBBONS ETC): ....

COST: ....

FLOWER PLANNER

BUTTONHOLES FOR:

_____

_____

_____

_____

CORSAGES FOR:

_____

_____

_____

....

notes

FLOWER PLANNER

CEREMONY FLOWERS

STYLE/SHAPE:

COLOUR SCHEME:

FLOWERS:

GREENERY:

OTHER (RIBBONS ETC):

COST:

LOCATIONS:

FLOWER PLANNER

RECEPTION FLOWERS

STYLE/SHAPE:

COLOUR SCHEME:

FLOWERS:

GREENERY:

OTHER (RIBBONS ETC):

COST:

LOCATIONS:

add flower inspiration here

RECEPTION

RECEPTION CHECKLIST

○ Consider the location of your reception venue in light of the season – if you are holding an event out of doors, even under cover of a marquee, you will need to anticipate weather conditions.

○ Does the style of venue reflect the type of wedding you want? If it is very grand and formal you may not feel relaxed and comfortable.

○ Consider what kind of food you want – a buffet, a seated meal or champagne and canapés? It will make a big difference to your budget.

○ Do you want an evening reception? This can be an opportunity to extend your guest list but then you will need to consider entertainment and other additional costs too.

○ If you would like dancing, is there space for a dance floor?

○ If you are inviting children do consider them in the arrangements. Is there somewhere they can play and let off steam? Do you want to lay on entertainment for them or offer a special menu?

○ Check out wedding packages on offer and whether these can be tailored to your specific requirements.

○ Find out if any other weddings are planned at the venue the same day. If there are, will the venue be able to cope?

○ Make sure you are aware of any restrictions in terms of noise, filming, dancing, naked flames etc.

○ Think about how your guests will arrive. Is there sufficient parking? Will guests be able to use public transport?

○ Find out how the room(s) will be decorated. Can you supply the decorations and if so, when would they need to be delivered by and at what time would the room be decorated?

○ Consider whether you will need to organise separate catering. This can give you more flexibility but it might mean more work for you.

O   Consider whether you can supply your own alcohol. This may be a lot cheaper but you will probably be charged a corkage fee so work it out carefully.

O   Find out if your venue can provide somewhere for the you and your partner to change if you need to (ideally free of charge).

O   Can your venue accommodate guests overnight? If so, will they offer a discount? Can they recommend accommodation locally?

O   Always ask for recent testimonials from previous weddings, or look for reviews online.

O   To avoid misunderstandings, agree everything in writing. Keep a copy of all correspondence, emails and notes of telephone conversations and meetings as well as quotations.

....

notes

QUESTIONS TO ASK THE VENUE

WHAT DATES AND TIMES ARE AVAILABLE?

WHAT ARE THE ROOM/VENUE HIRE FEES?

WHAT IS THE PAYMENT POLICY?

HOW MUCH IS THE DEPOSIT AND WHEN IS IT REQUIRED?

WHEN WOULD THE BALANCE BE DUE?

WHAT IS THE CANCELLATION POLICY?

ARE CREDIT CARDS ACCEPTED?

DOES THE FACILITY HAVE LIABILITY INSURANCE?

IS VAT/SALES TAX INCLUDED IN THE PRICES?

WHAT ALTERNATIVE ARRANGEMENTS CAN BE MADE IF THE WEATHER IS BAD?

WHAT IS THE MINIMUM & MAXIMUM NUMBER OF GUESTS ALLOWED?
FOR A SEATED RECEPTION?
FOR A COCKTAIL RECEPTION?

DOES THE VENUE HAVE IN-HOUSE CATERING?

CATERING: SEE SEPARATE CHECKLIST FOR CATERING & ADAPT THIS
ACCORDING TO WHETHER YOU ARE USING CATERERS SUPPLIED BY YOUR
VENUE OR BRINGING THEM IN SPECIALLY

CAN I BRING IN MY OWN SUPPLIERS?

IF SO, ARE THERE ANY RESTRICTIONS?

CAN YOU MAKE ANY RECOMMENDATIONS?

DO YOU OFFER A WEDDING PACKAGE OR CAN I CREATE MY OWN OR
ADAPT/MODIFY ONE OF YOURS?

WHAT MUSIC IS AVAILABLE ON SITE & AT WHAT COST?

WHAT RESTRICTIONS ON MUSIC ARE THERE, IF ANY?

WHAT PHOTOGRAPHY RESTRICTIONS ARE THERE, IF ANY?

WHAT POLICY IS THERE ON CONFETTI, RICE & PETAL THROWING?

WHAT POLICY IS THERE WITH REGARD TO CANDLES?

WHAT FLORAL & TABLE DECORATIONS ARE AVAILABLE & AT WHAT COST?

HOW MANY STAFF WILL BE AVAILABLE TO SERVE? WHAT WILL THEY WEAR?

WHAT PARKING IS AVAILABLE FOR GUESTS?

IS THERE A PARKING FEE?

IS THERE DISABLED ACCESS & PARKING?

WHAT PUBLIC TRANSPORT IS AVAILABLE FOR GUESTS?

WILL ANY OTHER EVENTS BE SCHEDULED ON THE SAME DAY & IF SO,
WHERE & AT WHAT TIME? HOW WILL THEY BE MANAGED?

WHAT ALCOHOL RESTRICTIONS ARE THERE, IF ANY?

notes

COMPARING

NAME:

ADDRESS:

WEBSITE:
EMAIL:
PHONE:

NAME:

ADDRESS:

WEBSITE:
EMAIL:
PHONE:

COMPARING

NAME: ADDRESS: WEBSITE: EMAIL: PHONE:	NAME: ADDRESS: WEBSITE: EMAIL: PHONE:

ARE YOU AVAILABLE ON MY CHOSEN DATE?

HOW MANY YEARS HAVE YOU BEEN IN BUSINESS?

WHAT IS THE PAYMENT POLICY?

HOW MUCH IS THE DEPOSIT AND WHEN IS IT REQUIRED?

WHEN WOULD THE BALANCE BE DUE?

WHAT IS THE CANCELLATION POLICY?

DO YOU HAVE LIABILITY INSURANCE?

WHEN IS THE FINAL HEAD-COUNT NEEDED?

DO YOU HAVE A SPECIALITY?

WHAT IS YOUR RATIO OF WAITING STAFF TO GUESTS?

WHAT IS THE DRESS CODE FOR WAITING STAFF?

DO YOU PROVIDE TABLE LINENS, GLASSWARE, CUTLERY ETC?
IF SO, CAN I CHOOSE COLOURS & DESIGNS?

IF WE HAVE TO HIRE CHINA, GLASSWARE & CUTLERY, WILL YOU CLEAN
& RETURN EVERYTHING?

HAVE YOU WORKED AT MY CHOSEN VENUE BEFORE?

ARE YOU ABLE TO BRING YOUR OWN COOKING FACILITIES OR CAN YOU USE
THE FACILITIES PROVIDED?

WHAT IS THE PRICE RANGE FOR A SEATED LUNCH/BUFFET LUNCH?

WHAT IS THE PRICE RANGE FOR A SEATED DINNER/BUFFET DINNER?

WHAT IS THE PRICE RANGE FOR CANAPÉS?

IS IT POSSIBLE TO SAMPLE THE MENU?

CAN YOU CATER FOR DIFFERENT DIETARY REQUIREMENTS?

WILL THERE BE MORE THAN ONE OPTION FOR GUESTS TO CHOOSE FROM?

CAN YOU OFFER SNACKS/FOOD IF THERE IS AN EVENING RECEPTION?

DO YOU OFFER ANY SPECIALITIES OR VARIATIONS ON THE TRADITIONAL
WEDDING BREAKFAST?

ARE YOU ABLE TO DECORATE THE TABLES?

CAN WE PROVIDE OUR OWN ALCOHOL? DO YOU CHARGE A CORKAGE FEE?

WHAT ALTERNATIVES CAN YOU OFFER IN THE WAY OF
NON-ALCOHOLIC DRINKS?

HOW MUCH GRATUITY IS EXPECTED?

CAN YOU GIVE ME AN ITEMISED BUDGET AND BILL?

IS THERE A CAKE-CUTTING FEE? IF SO, HOW MUCH IS IT?

IS THERE A BAR-TENDING FEE? IF SO, HOW MUCH IS IT?

IS THERE A CLEAN-UP FEE? IF SO, HOW MUCH IS IT?

ARE THERE ANY OTHER CHARGES RELATING TO THE CAKE OR THE MEAL
OR ANYTHING?

IS VAT INCLUDED IN THE PRICES QUOTED?

notes

COMPARING

NAME:	NAME:
ADDRESS:	ADDRESS:
WEBSITE:	WEBSITE:
EMAIL:	EMAIL:
PHONE:	PHONE:

COMPARING

NAME:	NAME:
ADDRESS:	ADDRESS:
WEBSITE: EMAIL: PHONE:	WEBSITE: EMAIL: PHONE:

VENUE & CATERER INFORMATION

VENUE NAME:

ADDRESS:

WEBSITE:

CONTACT NAME:

PHONE:

EMAIL:

ROOM

NAME OF ROOM(S):

ROOM CAPACITY:

AVAILABLE FROM: _____ TIME: _____

AVAILABLE UNTIL: _____ TIME: _____

DATE CONFIRMED:

CONFIRM HEAD COUNT BY:

COLOUR SCHEME:

TABLES:

LINENS:

FLOWERS:

TOTAL COST:

DEPOSIT: _____ DUE: _____ PAID: _____

BALANCE: _____ DUE: _____ PAID: _____

GRATUITIES:

CANCELLATION POLICY:

CATERER'S NAME:

ADDRESS:

WEBSITE:

CONTACT NAME:

PHONE:

EMAIL:

COST

COST PER HEAD: _____ (ADULT) _____ (CHILD)

TOTAL COST:

DEPOSIT: _____ DUE: _____ PAID: _____

BALANCE: _____ DUE: _____ PAID: _____

GRATUITIES:

CANCELLATION POLICY:

TIMETABLE

GUESTS ARRIVE:

BRIDE & GROOM ARRIVE:

CHAMPAGNE/DRINKS & CANAPÉS:

FOOD IS SERVED:

SPEECHES:

CAKE:

AFTERNOON RECEPTION ENDS:

EVENING RECEPTION BEGINS:

BRIDE & GROOM LEAVE:

RECEPTION ROOM TO BE VACATED BY:

DRINKS PLANNER

NUMBER OF GUESTS (RECEPTION): _____ (EVENING): _____

NUMBER OF CHILDREN (RECEPTION): _____ (EVENING): _____

ON ARRIVAL

_____ NUMBER OF BOTTLES: _____ PRICE: _____

_____ NUMBER OF BOTTLES: _____ PRICE: _____

_____ NUMBER OF BOTTLES: _____ PRICE: _____

NON-ALCOHOLIC

_____ NUMBER OF BOTTLES: _____ PRICE: _____

_____ NUMBER OF BOTTLES: _____ PRICE: _____

MEAL

_____ NUMBER OF BOTTLES: _____ PRICE: _____

_____ NUMBER OF BOTTLES: _____ PRICE: _____

_____ NUMBER OF BOTTLES: _____ PRICE: _____

NON-ALCOHOLIC

_____ NUMBER OF BOTTLES: _____ PRICE: _____

_____ NUMBER OF BOTTLES: _____ PRICE: _____

EVENING

_____ NUMBER OF BOTTLES: _____ PRICE: _____

_____ NUMBER OF BOTTLES: _____ PRICE: _____

_____ NUMBER OF BOTTLES: _____ PRICE: _____

NON-ALCOHOLIC

_____ NUMBER OF BOTTLES: _____ PRICE: _____

_____ NUMBER OF BOTTLES: _____ PRICE: _____

notes

....

tip

If you want to put an amount behind the bar for drinks perhaps nominate
a responsible person (preferably one who won't be drinking) to sign off with
the bar staff at agreed amounts and keep an eye on things generally and your
generosity will probably go further.

○   Have you got a theme for the wedding that you want carried through into the menu?

○   Have you got children attending, and if so, will they need a special menu?

○   Have you got a vegetarian and vegan option?

○   Do you need to cater for any other special dietary needs?

○   If you are doing the wedding photographs straight after the ceremony do you want to give your guests some canapés to have with their welcome drinks? Photographs always take longer than you think and many people don't like drinking on an empty stomach.

○   Will your caterer allow you to sample different menus?

○   If your reception is continuing into the evening do you want to have more food later on? Remember, some guests may only be coming in the evening.

○   If you are having a buffet don't assume people will choose between main course options. People like to try a bit of everything so unless you give specific instructions to your guests you need to take this account when ordering your food or you will run out.

○   Find out what the venue/caterer's policy is if the food does run out – will they be able to supplement with something else?

notes

MENU OPTION 1

COST PER HEAD: .... TOTAL COST: ....

COMMENTS: ....

....

....

....

....

....

....

MENU OPTION 2

COST PER HEAD: .... TOTAL COST: ....

COMMENTS: ....

....

....

....

....

....

....

MENU OPTION 3

COST PER HEAD: .... TOTAL COST: ....

COMMENTS: ....

....

....

....

....

....

....

FINAL AGREED MENU

COST PER HEAD: .... TOTAL COST: ....

DATE CONFIRMED: ....

DETAILS: ....

....

....

....

....

....

....

....

....

....

....

....

....

....

....

....

....

....

....

....

....

....

....

....

....

....

....

....

....

TABLE DECORATIONS

○   Colour scheme?

○   Centrepieces? Make sure any centrepieces are low enough to allow your guests to talk easily to each other across the table. The top table traditionally has a larger centrepiece.

○   Favours? Party favours are little gift items given to guests as a memento. These can range from traditional sugared almonds in net twists to more elaborate, customized gifts. If you are looking to save some money this is an area where it's easy to make cutbacks.

○   Candles? Check first whether your venue allows a naked flame.

○   Balloons? These always look festive but don't make plans to release them without checking with your venue as it could be against the law.

○   Disposable cameras? Placing these on tables is a great way to get informal shots. Deputise one of the attendants to collect them at the end of the night.

○   Place names? Do you want to seat your guests or let them choose where to sit? If you are seating your guests you will need a master seating plan so guests can find their place as well as place cards on the tables. Discuss this with your venue.

....

notes

ENTERTAINMENT

You might have live music at your reception or you might simply have some background music from a playlist of your choice. You may go on to have an evening reception with dancing. Whatever you have planned, the type of music you want will vary at different times of the day. Don't underestimate the importance of music/entertainment. Think of your wedding in terms of a big party. If you are having live music or a DJ you may like to consider the following:

O   Discuss the playlist. You will want to create a good atmosphere and entertain all age groups. You may want the music to reflect the theme of your day. The DJ or band should be able to provide a standard list but don't be afraid to make some special requests – particularly if there is a song or songs that have a particular meaning for you. Always let them know special requests in advance.

O   Discuss the first dance and what music you would like.

O   Can they provide references and testimonials or can you find them online?

O   What will happen on the day? Make sure they are organised and will sort themselves out in terms of setting up, parking etc.

O   Check out what is included and make sure you have everything detailed and confirmed in writing.

O   Do they have a cancellation clause and if so, what are their terms?

O   If you are bringing a laptop, MP3 player or CDs to the venue, make sure someone is responsible for picking them up at the end of the evening or make arrangements to pick them up after the reception.

notes

Photocopy these pages as many times as you like to get the required number of tables and shapes. Cut up a printed list of guests' names and then play around with placing people on different tables and in varying configurations until you are happy. Only then pencil in the actual table numbers with names. However, there is no point in doing this until you have finalized your guest list.

O   How many copies of the seating plan do you need to supply to the venue?

O   Are you having place cards on the table or letting guests seat themselves?

O   If you have small children coming, perhaps position them and their parents so they can leave the room easily if necessary.

O   It can be nice to mix up guests from both sides of the wedding party so they can get to know each other.

O   You will need to find out from your venue what shape your tables are and their capacity.

TOP TABLE

TABLE NO.

SEATING PLAN

TABLE NO.

TABLE NO.

TABLE NO.

TABLE NO.

TABLE NO.

TABLE NO.

SEATING PLAN

TABLE NO.

TABLE NO.

TABLE NO.

TABLE NO.

TABLE NO.

TABLE NO.

QUESTIONS TO ASK THE CAKE SUPPLIER

HOW MANY YEARS HAVE YOU BEEN IN BUSINESS?

WHAT ARE YOUR SPECIALITIES?

WHAT IS THE PAYMENT POLICY (DEPOSIT AMOUNT/BALANCE DUE ETC?)

WHAT IS YOUR CANCELLATION POLICY?

DO YOU ACCEPT CREDIT CARDS?

CAN YOU GIVE ME A COST PER SERVING?

HOW FAR IN ADVANCE SHOULD I CONFIRM?

DO YOU DELIVER?

WHEN WOULD YOU DELIVER THE CAKE?

CAN THE CAKE BE COLLECTED?

IS THERE A SET-UP FEE?

DO YOU LEND, RENT OR SELL CAKE STANDS & KNIVES? IF SO, WHAT IS THE
COST AND WHAT DEPOSIT IS REQUIRED?

WHEN DO THESE ITEMS HAVE TO BE RETURNED?

WHAT TYPES OF CAKE COULD I HAVE?

DO YOU OFFER FREE TASTINGS OF YOUR CAKES?

DO YOU CATER FOR ALLERGIES EG. NUT OR GLUTEN-FREE CAKES?

ARE YOUR CAKES FROZEN OR FRESH?

CAN YOU MAKE A CAKE TO MY DESIGN OR COPY ONE I HAVE
SEEN ELSEWHERE?

MY FRIEND/RELATIVE WANTS TO BAKE THE CAKE, CAN YOU DECORATE IT?

DO YOU SELL CAKE BOXES?

collect your ideas here

COMPARING

NAME: ADDRESS: WEBSITE: EMAIL: PHONE:	NAME: ADDRESS: WEBSITE: EMAIL: PHONE:

COMPARING

NAME:

ADDRESS:

WEBSITE:
EMAIL:
PHONE:

NAME:

ADDRESS:

WEBSITE:
EMAIL:
PHONE:

FINAL CAKE DESIGN & DETAILS

CHOSEN CAKE SUPPLIER:

FINAL CAKE COST: _____ DUE: _____/_____/_____

DEPOSIT AMOUNT: _____ DUE: _____/_____/_____

FINAL CAKE DESIGN:

FINAL CAKE FLAVOURS:

DATE CAKE WILL BE READY:

DATE TO COLLECT CAKE/HAVE DELIVERED:

FINAL CAKE DESIGN NOTES:

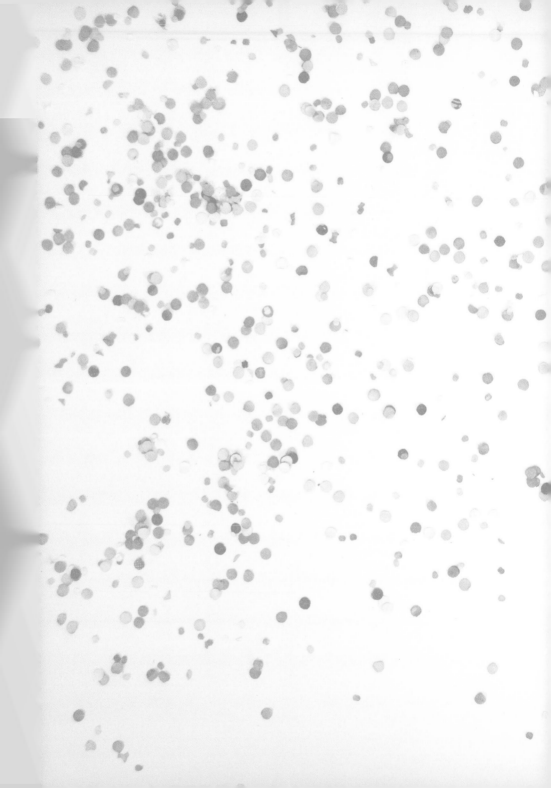

GUESTS

O   Guest list (Ceremony) finalized

O   Guest list (Afternoon Reception) finalized

O   Guest list (Evening Reception) finalized

O   Full addresses and post codes collected

O   Invitations sent out (include directions and response cards and accommodation options if needed)

O   Provisional numbers given to caterers etc

O   Confirmed numbers given to caterers etc

tip

+ Always order extra invitations and envelopes so you don't run short if you make a mistake or need a last-minute invite.
+ Address a few invitations at a time to make it easier to get through them, but don't send them out until all are done otherwise some people may think they have been forgotten or are on a 'b' list.
+ Spread the word about the date among family and friends as soon as possible.
+ Be clear about what your policy is regarding children attending from the start. If you can't accommodate children say so in an enclosed note with the invitation to avoid misunderstandings.
+ Include directions to the venue and accommodation options if needed with the invites.
+ Be sensitive to the fact that your guests will be on different budgets and suggest accommodation within a range of price brackets.
+ Agree where responses are coming to and who is going to keep track of RSVPs. You don't want to have to pay for no-shows if it can be avoided. Give an email address if you want to be sure of a quick response.

GUEST LIST

NAME	NO. OF ADULTS	NO. OF CHILDREN	CEREMONY	RECEPTION	EVENING PARTY	RSVP
SUB TOTAL TO BE CARRIED FORWARD						

GUEST LIST

NAME	NO. OF ADULTS	NO. OF CHILDREN	CEREMONY	RECEPTION	EVENING PARTY	RSVP
SUB TOTAL TO BE CARRIED FORWARD						

GUEST LIST

NAME	NO. OF ADULTS	NO. OF CHILDREN	CEREMONY	RECEPTION	EVENING PARTY	RSVP
SUB TOTAL TO BE CARRIED FORWARD						

GUEST LIST

NAME	NO. OF ADULTS	NO. OF CHILDREN	CEREMONY	RECEPTION	EVENING PARTY	RSVP
SUB TOTAL TO BE CARRIED FORWARD						

GUEST LIST

NAME	NO. OF ADULTS	NO. OF CHILDREN	CEREMONY	RECEPTION	EVENING PARTY	RSVP
SUB TOTAL TO BE CARRIED FORWARD						

GUEST LIST

NAME	NO. OF ADULTS	NO. OF CHILDREN	CEREMONY	RECEPTION	EVENING PARTY	RSVP
SUB TOTAL TO BE CARRIED FORWARD						

GUEST LIST

NAME	NO. OF ADULTS	NO. OF CHILDREN	CEREMONY	RECEPTION	EVENING PARTY	RSVP
SUB TOTAL TO BE CARRIED FORWARD						

GUEST LIST

NAME	NO. OF ADULTS	NO. OF CHILDREN	CEREMONY	RECEPTION	EVENING PARTY	RSVP
SUB TOTAL TO BE CARRIED FORWARD						

GUEST LIST

NAME	NO. OF ADULTS	NO. OF CHILDREN	CEREMONY	RECEPTION	EVENING PARTY	RSVP
SUB TOTAL TO BE CARRIED FORWARD						

GUEST LIST

NAME	NO. OF ADULTS	NO. OF CHILDREN	CEREMONY	RECEPTION	EVENING PARTY	RSVP
SUB TOTAL TO BE CARRIED FORWARD						

SUMMARY OF CONFIRMED ATTENDEES

CEREMONY

VENUE NEEDS FINAL CONFIRMATION OF NUMBERS BY:

NUMBER OF ADULTS:

NUMBER OF CHILDREN:

SPECIAL NEEDS/ACCESS:

WEDDING BREAKFAST

VENUE NEEDS FINAL CONFIRMATION OF NUMBERS BY:

NUMBER OF ADULTS:

NUMBER OF CHILDREN:

SPECIAL NEEDS/ACCESS:

EVENING RECEPTION

VENUE NEEDS FINAL CONFIRMATION OF NUMBERS BY:

NUMBER OF ADULTS:

NUMBER OF CHILDREN:

SPECIAL NEEDS/ACCESS:

Often weddings are an occasion for family members to travel from distant parts of the globe. So whether you have people flying in from another country or catching a train from another town, be prepared for arranging pick-ups and accommodation. You can delegate as much as possible but keep on top of who is arriving when in the following pages.

NAME:

ARRIVAL DATE: TIME:

FLIGHT/TRAIN INFO:

BEING PICKED UP BY: AT:

WILL STAY AT:

NOTES:

NAME:

ARRIVAL DATE: TIME:

FLIGHT/TRAIN INFO:

BEING PICKED UP BY: AT:

WILL STAY AT:

NOTES:

NAME:

ARRIVAL DATE: TIME:

FLIGHT/TRAIN INFO:

BEING PICKED UP BY: AT:

WILL STAY AT:

NOTES:

NAME:

ARRIVAL DATE: TIME:

FLIGHT/TRAIN INFO:

BEING PICKED UP BY: AT:

WILL STAY AT:

NOTES:

NAME:

ARRIVAL DATE: TIME:

FLIGHT/TRAIN INFO:

BEING PICKED UP BY: AT:

WILL STAY AT:

NOTES:

NAME:

ARRIVAL DATE: TIME:

FLIGHT/TRAIN INFO:

BEING PICKED UP BY: AT:

WILL STAY AT:

NOTES:

NAME:

ARRIVAL DATE: TIME:

FLIGHT/TRAIN INFO:

BEING PICKED UP BY: AT:

WILL STAY AT:

NOTES:

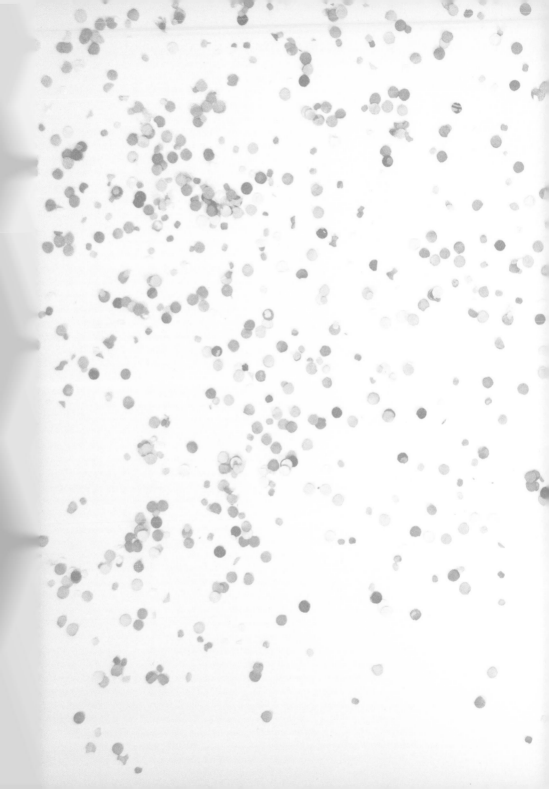

STATIONERY

STATIONERY CHECKLIST

Stationery is an area where it's possible to spend lots of money – the flip side is that it is also an area where you can make savings if you are on a budget. Decide early on what you really want to provide in the way of stationery and shop around for the best deals, or even consider designing your own (although cost it out carefully – buying 'off the shelf' could work out cheaper than having something you've designed specially printed).

○ Postage in the UK is calculated on size as well as weight so if you are on a budget check the guidelines before committing to a particular size – a small difference in size may save you money.

○ Make sure you order enough of everything – plus a few extra in case of mistakes. Remember that you don't need an invitation for every person – just for every couple or family – but you probably do want an Order of Service for everyone (plus any extras at the ceremony such as musicians, officiator etc).

○ Always include a cut-off date for RSVPs (and the address or email they should go to) otherwise you could end up paying for people who don't turn up.

○ If you are on a budget, be realistic: maps and cards with alternative arrangements in case of rain can always be photocopies rather than specially printed, or you could consider creating a wedding website which includes this information.

YOU MAY WANT TO ORDER THE FOLLOWING:

○ Invitations and envelopes (for ceremony and reception)

○ Response cards/envelopes

○ Reception cards and envelopes (include if you are inviting people to the reception only)

○ Evening reception cards and envelopes (include if you are inviting people to a separate evening reception)

○ Ceremony cards and envelopes (if the guest list for the reception is more than the ceremony itself you will need separate ceremony cards)

○ Rain cards (if the ceremony/reception is outdoors and you have an alternative lined up in case of bad weather)

- Maps (always have some extra for the ushers to hand out after the ceremony)

- Order of Service

- Seating/place cards (for the reception)

- Thank-you notes and envelopes

- Stamps (invitations)

- Stamps (response cards)

- Stamps (thank-you notes)

- Calligraphy pens

....

notes

QUESTIONS TO ASK THE STATIONERY SUPPLIER

WHAT ARE YOUR PAYMENT TERMS?

WHAT IS THE LEAD TIME REQUIRED?

WHAT IS YOUR CANCELLATION POLICY?

DO YOU OFFER A MONEY-BACK GUARANTEE?

DO YOU OFFER A DESIGN SERVICE?

CAN YOU PRINT TO MY DESIGN?

WHAT FORMAT WOULD YOU NEED ARTWORK IN?

DO YOU OFFER ANY WEDDING PACKAGES?

WILL I BE ABLE TO APPROVE A PROOF BEFORE PRINTING?

QUOTE FOR INVITATIONS & ENVELOPES:

QUOTE FOR RESPONSE CARDS & ENVELOPES:

QUOTE FOR RECEPTION CARDS:

QUOTE FOR CEREMONY CARDS:

QUOTE FOR SEATING/PLACE CARDS:

QUOTE FOR MAPS:

QUOTE FOR ORDER OF SERVICE:

QUOTE FOR THANK YOU NOTES & ENVELOPES:

tip

When you are asking for quotes be consistent in what you are asking for in terms of numbers, paper quality etc so you can truly compare costs.

sketch your ideas here

COMPARING

NAME: ADDRESS: WEBSITE: EMAIL: PHONE:	NAME: ADDRESS: WEBSITE: EMAIL: PHONE:

COMPARING

NAME: ADDRESS: WEBSITE: EMAIL: PHONE:	NAME: ADDRESS: WEBSITE: EMAIL: PHONE:

STATIONERY SUMMARY

ITEM	QUANTITY	BUDGETED COST	ACTUAL COST
INVITATIONS & ENVELOPES			
RESPONSE CARDS & ENVELOPES			
RECEPTION CARDS & ENVELOPES			
CEREMONY CARDS & ENVELOPES			
SEATING/ PLACE CARDS			
RAIN CARDS			
MAPS			
ORDER OF SERVICE			
THANK YOU NOTES & ENVELOPES			
STAMPS (REMEMBER TO BUDGET FOR ANY OVERSEAS STAMPS TOO)			
PHOTOCOPYING			
CALLIGRAPHY			
TOTAL			

STATIONERY SUPPLIER

STORE NAME:

ADDRESS:

WEBSITE:

PHONE:

EMAIL:

DESCRIPTION:

DEPOSIT DUE: _____   PAID: _____

BALANCE DUE: _____   PAID: _____

STATIONERY ORDERING TIMELINE

FINAL DESIGN TO BE CHOSEN BY:

FINAL WORDING TO BE AGREED BY:

FINAL QUANTITY TO BE AGREED BY:

PROOF DUE:

DELIVERY BY:

SUMMARY OF ORDER

GIFTS

THE WEDDING LIST

Wedding lists can be very helpful – many guests really would like to buy a gift that is wanted but it can be difficult to know what a couple already has, particularly if they have been living together. However, there are always going to be some people who prefer to do their own thing and buy off-list. Only you will know whether you feel comfortable about putting details of the list in with the invitations or whether it would be more appropriate to let people ask.

- You can have wedding lists in as many different places as you like and many speciality shops now offer a wedding list service.

- Some online wedding services are not tied to a particular store.

- Make sure you are using an established service and check out how your gifts will be protected if the business runs into trouble.

- Try and finalize your list before your invitations are sent, that is, approximately 3 months before the wedding date. You can usually add items to your list at any time but check this out in advance.

- Many lists now run online options so if this is important to you double-check in advance what can be done online and what can't.

- Make sure you include a good range of items so there are some less expensive items on your list but remember that some people, for example, work colleagues, may like to club together to buy you something more expensive.

- Check out what delivery options are on offer and how frequent they are, and what, if anything, you will be charged.

- Find out how guests can buy off the list – not everyone will have access to the internet.

- Find out when your list will be closed. Six weeks after the wedding is common.

- Check if your guests can include messages with gifts – some companies offer it but others don't so it depends how important this is to you.

- Find out if they will give you a card to send out with your invitations (it will save you having to make one).

- Check if you will you be able to swap items once the list is closed.

- If you prefer not to send out details of the wedding list with your invitations make sure key people such as your parents or attendants have all the information to hand so they can send it out easily on request.

- Your wedding list provider may send you regular updates but it is always a good idea to check the list regularly to see whether you need to add more things.

- If you've been living together for a while you may decide that there is little you need and you don't want a wedding list but there are other options: you can always ask for store vouchers instead, some holiday companies allow contributions to the honeymoon and guests can pay for specific elements, also many charities would welcome donations. Whatever you decide to do be as clear about it as you can so there are no misunderstandings and your guests won't be embarrassed if they haven't bought you a gift.

- If you do ask for vouchers or money do try and let the giver know specifically what you will be spending the money on when you write your thank you note.

- Choose items on your list together and make sure there is something there for both of you to enjoy.

....

notes

WEDDING LIST PROVIDER

NAME:

ADDRESS:

PHONE:

EMAIL:

GIFT LIST NUMBER:

GIFT LIST PASSWORD:

GIFT LIST 'GUEST' PASSWORD:

NAME:

ADDRESS:

PHONE:

EMAIL:

GIFT LIST NUMBER:

GIFT LIST PASSWORD:

GIFT LIST 'GUEST' PASSWORD:

NAME:

ADDRESS:

PHONE:

EMAIL:

GIFT LIST NUMBER:

GIFT LIST PASSWORD:

GIFT LIST 'GUEST' PASSWORD:

GIFTS RECEIVED & THANK YOU NOTES SENT

NAME:

GIFT:

O   THANK YOU NOTE SENT?

NAME:

GIFT:

O   THANK YOU NOTE SENT?

NAME:

GIFT:

O   THANK YOU NOTE SENT?

NAME:

GIFT:

O   THANK YOU NOTE SENT?

NAME:

GIFT:

O   THANK YOU NOTE SENT?

NAME:

GIFT:

O   THANK YOU NOTE SENT?

NAME:

GIFT:

O   THANK YOU NOTE SENT?

NAME:

GIFT:

O   THANK YOU NOTE SENT?

NAME:

GIFT:

O   THANK YOU NOTE SENT?

NAME:

GIFT:

O   THANK YOU NOTE SENT?

NAME:

GIFT:

O   THANK YOU NOTE SENT?

NAME:

GIFT:

O   THANK YOU NOTE SENT?

GIFTS RECEIVED & THANK YOU NOTES SENT

NAME: ....

GIFT: ....

○   THANK YOU NOTE SENT?

NAME: ....

GIFT: ....

○   THANK YOU NOTE SENT?

NAME: ....

GIFT: ....

○   THANK YOU NOTE SENT?

NAME: ....

GIFT: ....

○   THANK YOU NOTE SENT?

NAME: ....

GIFT: ....

○   THANK YOU NOTE SENT?

NAME: ....

GIFT: ....

○   THANK YOU NOTE SENT?

NAME: ....

GIFT: ....

○   THANK YOU NOTE SENT?

NAME: ....

GIFT: ....

○   THANK YOU NOTE SENT?

NAME: ....

GIFT: ....

○   THANK YOU NOTE SENT?

NAME: ....

GIFT: ....

○   THANK YOU NOTE SENT?

NAME: ....

GIFT: ....

○   THANK YOU NOTE SENT?

NAME: ....

GIFT: ....

○   THANK YOU NOTE SENT?

GIFTS RECEIVED & THANK YOU NOTES SENT

NAME: ....

GIFT: ....

○ THANK YOU NOTE SENT?

NAME: ....

GIFT: ....

○ THANK YOU NOTE SENT?

NAME: ....

GIFT: ....

○ THANK YOU NOTE SENT?

NAME: ....

GIFT: ....

○ THANK YOU NOTE SENT?

NAME: ....

GIFT: ....

○ THANK YOU NOTE SENT?

NAME: ....

GIFT: ....

○ THANK YOU NOTE SENT?

NAME: ....

GIFT: ....

○ THANK YOU NOTE SENT?

NAME: ....

GIFT: ....

○ THANK YOU NOTE SENT?

NAME: ....

GIFT: ....

○ THANK YOU NOTE SENT?

NAME: ....

GIFT: ....

○ THANK YOU NOTE SENT?

NAME: ....

GIFT: ....

○ THANK YOU NOTE SENT?

NAME: ....

GIFT: ....

○ THANK YOU NOTE SENT?

GIFTS RECEIVED & THANK YOU NOTES SENT

NAME:

GIFT:

○ THANK YOU NOTE SENT?

NAME:

GIFT:

○ THANK YOU NOTE SENT?

NAME:

GIFT:

○ THANK YOU NOTE SENT?

NAME:

GIFT:

○ THANK YOU NOTE SENT?

NAME:

GIFT:

○ THANK YOU NOTE SENT?

NAME:

GIFT:

○ THANK YOU NOTE SENT?

NAME:

GIFT:

○ THANK YOU NOTE SENT?

NAME:

GIFT:

○ THANK YOU NOTE SENT?

NAME:

GIFT:

○ THANK YOU NOTE SENT?

NAME:

GIFT:

○ THANK YOU NOTE SENT?

NAME:

GIFT:

○ THANK YOU NOTE SENT?

NAME:

GIFT:

○ THANK YOU NOTE SENT?

GIFTS RECEIVED & THANK YOU NOTES SENT

NAME:

GIFT:

O   THANK YOU NOTE SENT?

NAME:

GIFT:

O   THANK YOU NOTE SENT?

NAME:

GIFT:

O   THANK YOU NOTE SENT?

NAME:

GIFT:

O   THANK YOU NOTE SENT?

NAME:

GIFT:

O   THANK YOU NOTE SENT?

NAME:

GIFT:

O   THANK YOU NOTE SENT?

NAME:

GIFT:

O   THANK YOU NOTE SENT?

NAME:

GIFT:

O   THANK YOU NOTE SENT?

NAME:

GIFT:

O   THANK YOU NOTE SENT?

NAME:

GIFT:

O   THANK YOU NOTE SENT?

NAME:

GIFT:

O   THANK YOU NOTE SENT?

NAME:

GIFT:

O   THANK YOU NOTE SENT?

GIFTS RECEIVED & THANK YOU NOTES SENT

NAME:

GIFT:

○ THANK YOU NOTE SENT?

NAME:

GIFT:

○ THANK YOU NOTE SENT?

NAME:

GIFT:

○ THANK YOU NOTE SENT?

NAME:

GIFT:

○ THANK YOU NOTE SENT?

NAME:

GIFT:

○ THANK YOU NOTE SENT?

NAME:

GIFT:

○ THANK YOU NOTE SENT?

NAME:

GIFT:

○ THANK YOU NOTE SENT?

NAME:

GIFT:

○ THANK YOU NOTE SENT?

NAME:

GIFT:

○ THANK YOU NOTE SENT?

NAME:

GIFT:

○ THANK YOU NOTE SENT?

NAME:

GIFT:

○ THANK YOU NOTE SENT?

NAME:

GIFT:

○ THANK YOU NOTE SENT?

GIFTS RECEIVED & THANK YOU NOTES SENT

NAME:

GIFT:

○ THANK YOU NOTE SENT?

NAME:

GIFT:

○ THANK YOU NOTE SENT?

NAME:

GIFT:

○ THANK YOU NOTE SENT?

NAME:

GIFT:

○ THANK YOU NOTE SENT?

NAME:

GIFT:

○ THANK YOU NOTE SENT?

NAME:

GIFT:

○ THANK YOU NOTE SENT?

NAME:

GIFT:

○ THANK YOU NOTE SENT?

NAME:

GIFT:

○ THANK YOU NOTE SENT?

NAME:

GIFT:

○ THANK YOU NOTE SENT?

NAME:

GIFT:

○ THANK YOU NOTE SENT?

NAME:

GIFT:

○ THANK YOU NOTE SENT?

NAME:

GIFT:

○ THANK YOU NOTE SENT?

GIFTS TO BUY

Here is a suggested list of gifts often given by the bride and groom at a traditional wedding:

- ○ Bridesmaids' gifts given by the bride

- ○ Flower girls and pageboys gifts given by the bride

- ○ Chief bridesmaid's gift given by the bride

- ○ Ushers' gifts given by the groom

- ○ Best man's gift given by the groom

- ○ Bride's gift to the groom

- ○ Groom's gift to the bride

Or make your own list of gifts you'd like to give:

PHOTOGRAPHY

Having a record of your day is so important – the day flies by and you can't be everywhere at once so being able to re-live and see what else was going on through photographs and/or film will give you hours of pleasure.

O   Be wary of asking an enthusiastic amateur to do your photos/filming –
     if anything goes wrong it's virtually impossible to re-create the day.

O   Think about the style of photography you want – traditional, posed images or a
     fluid reportage style? The latter has become increasingly popular but it takes an
     excellent photographer to produce good shots through the whole day. Ask your
     photographer about their style – it's quite hard for them to do both so be clear
     about what you are asking for.

O   Look at albums of different photographers when you are comparing quotes –
     and it is worth going through the whole album to check for consistency.

O   Make sure you feel comfortable with the photographer. Meet them before you
     confirm. You want to be confident they will organise guests and family and be a
     calm creative presence.

O   Remember the photographer always owns copyright of the images so make sure
     you clarify early on what is included in the package in the way of reprints and
     what they will cost.

O   Always ask for a breakdown of costs in writing from both the photographer
     and the videographer.

O   Book your photographer as soon as you can – the good ones get booked up
     a long time in advance particularly during the wedding season.

O   When choosing a videographer, make sure you see a complete sample of their
     work rather than edited highlights.

O   Make sure the job is not being sub-contracted out.

O   Make sure you tell the photographer and/or videographer in advance if there
     are any key shots you want.

○ Feel free to suggest what music you want used in the film.

○ If you are getting a friend or relative to film the wedding, be realistic about what you might end up with.

....

notes

QUESTIONS TO ASK POTENTIAL PHOTOGRAPHERS

ARE YOU AVAILABLE ON MY CHOSEN DATE?

WHAT ARE YOUR FEES?

IS THERE A COST PER HOUR BEYOND THE AGREED TIME, AND IF SO, HOW MUCH IS IT?

WHAT ARE YOUR PAYMENT TERMS?

WHAT IS YOUR CANCELLATION POLICY?

DO YOU OFFER A MONEY-BACK GUARANTEE?

DO YOU HAVE PROFESSIONAL INDEMNITY INSURANCE?

WHAT IS YOUR EXPERIENCE OF PHOTOGRAPHING WEDDINGS?

WHAT STYLE OF PHOTOGRAPHS DO YOU TAKE (TRADITIONAL OR REPORTAGE)?

DO YOU HAVE ANY RECENT TESTIMONIALS FROM WEDDING CUSTOMERS?

WOULD YOU BE THE ACTUAL PHOTOGRAPHER ON THE DAY?

DO YOU BRING AN ASSISTANT?

DO YOU USE A DIGITAL OR FILM CAMERA?

DO YOU WORK IN BLACK & WHITE AND/OR COLOUR?

DO YOU BRING BACK UP EQUIPMENT WITH YOU ON THE DAY?

DO YOU VISIT THE CEREMONY OR RECEPTION VENUE BEFORE THE DAY?

DO YOU DO STUDIO PORTRAITS? AT WHAT COST?

CAN YOU DO RE-TOUCHING IF NECESSARY?

WHAT DIFFERENT WEDDING PACKAGES DO YOU OFFER?

CAN NEGATIVES BY PURCHASED AND IF SO, AT WHAT COST?

DO YOU USE PROOFS?

HOW MANY PROOFS WILL I GET AND WHEN?

IS IT POSSIBLE TO PURCHASE PROOFS?

WHAT IS YOUR RANGE OF ALBUMS & COST?

WHEN WILL I GET MY ALBUM?

WHAT IS THE COST OF A REPRINT – 5" X 7"? 8" X 10"? 11" X 14"?

DO YOU POST PICTURES ON A WEBSITE FOR FAMILY & FRIENDS TO ORDER?

COMPARING

NAME:	NAME:
ADDRESS:	ADDRESS:
WEBSITE: EMAIL: PHONE:	WEBSITE: EMAIL: PHONE:

COMPARING

NAME: ADDRESS: WEBSITE: EMAIL: PHONE:	NAME: ADDRESS: WEBSITE: EMAIL: PHONE:

PHOTOGRAPHER'S CONFIRMATION

COMPANY NAME:

ADDRESS:

WEBSITE:

CONTACT NAME:

PHONE:

EMAIL:

NAME OF PHOTOGRAPHER:

NAME OF ASSISTANT:

AGREED TIMETABLE ON THE DAY:

BOOKING CONFIRMED: _____ CONTACT: _____

COST:

DEPOSIT: _____ (DUE) _____ (PAID)

BALANCE: _____ (DUE) _____ (PAID)

AGREED PHOTOGRAPHS/ALBUMS (QUANTITY & COST)

WEDDING PHOTO PLANNER

Your photographer will want to know what photographs you want taken on the day so discuss this with your fiancé and both families. Copy this checklist and give it to your photographer to ensure nothing gets forgotten. If you want specific locations or other elements just write the details in the notes section but do make sure you have discussed these with the photographer beforehand. Some things just may not be logistically possible.

REMEMBER

+ The more photographs you can have taken before the ceremony the better.
+ Plan what your guests will be doing while photographs are being taken.
+ The list below offers some guidance but you can have whatever photographs taken that you wish. Informal photos are fun too!
+ Make sure you tell the photographer and/or videographer in advance if there are any key shots you want.
+ Feel free to suggest what music you want used in the film.
+ If you are getting a friend or relative to film the wedding, be realistic about what you might end up with.

PRE-CEREMONY PHOTOGRAPHS

○ _____

○ _____

○ _____

○ _____

○ _____

○ _____

○ _____

○ _____

○ _____

WEDDING PHOTO PLANNER

CEREMONY PHOTOGRAPHS

- ○
- ○
- ○
- ○
- ○
- ○
- ○

POST-CEREMONY PHOTOGRAPHS

- ○
- ○
- ○
- ○
- ○
- ○

RECEPTION PHOTOGRAPHS

- ○
- ○
- ○

○ _____

○ _____

○ _____

○ _____

○ _____

○ _____

○ _____

○ _____

○ _____

○ _____

○ _____

○ _____

OTHER IDEAS

○ _____

○ _____

○ _____

○ _____

○ _____

○ _____

○ _____

QUESTIONS TO ASK POTENTIAL VIDEOGRAPHERS

ARE YOU AVAILABLE ON MY CHOSEN DATE?

WHAT ARE YOUR FEES?

IS THERE A COST PER HOUR BEYOND THE AGREED TIME, AND IF SO, HOW MUCH IS IT?

WHAT ARE YOUR PAYMENT TERMS?

WHAT IS YOUR CANCELLATION POLICY?

DO YOU OFFER A MONEY-BACK GUARANTEE?

WHAT IS YOUR EXPERIENCE OF DOING WEDDING VIDEOS?

DO YOU HAVE ANY TESTIMONIALS FROM WEDDING CUSTOMERS?

WOULD YOU BE DOING THE FILMING ON THE DAY?

WOULD YOU BRING AN ASSITANT?

WHAT FORMAT DO YOU USE?

WHAT TYPE OF EQUIPMENT DO YOU USE? DO YOU HAVE A WIRELESS MICROPHONE?

DO YOU BRING BACK-UP EQUIPMENT WITH YOU ON THE DAY?

DO YOU VISIT THE CEREMONY/RECEPTION VENUE BEFORE THE DAY?

DO YOU EDIT THE TAPE AFTER THE EVENT? WHAT HAPPENS TO THE RAW FOOTAGE?

WHAT ABOUT MUSIC & CAPTIONS?

WHEN WILL I RECEIVE THE FINAL VIDEO?

WHAT IS THE COST OF YOUR WEDDING PACKAGE AND WHAT DOES IT INCLUDE?

CAN YOU MAKE A PHOTO MONTAGE AND IF SO, AT WHAT COST?

tip

Make sure you check beforehand with your officiator about what restrictions there are for filming. Sometimes it is preferred that the ceremony itself not be filmed.

NAME:	NAME:
ADDRESS:	ADDRESS:
WEBSITE: EMAIL: PHONE:	WEBSITE: EMAIL: PHONE:

VIDEOGRAPHER'S CONFIRMATION

COMPANY NAME:

ADDRESS:

WEBSITE:

CONTACT NAME:

PHONE:

EMAIL:

NAME OF VIDEOGRAPHER:

NAME OF ASSISTANT:

AGREED TIMETABLE ON THE DAY:

BOOKING CONFIRMED: _____ CONTACT: _____

COST:

DEPOSIT: _____ (DUE) _____ (PAID)

BALANCE: _____ (DUE) _____ (PAID)

DETAILS OF ANY FILMING RESTRICTIONS:

AGREED EDITING DETAILS:

TRANSPORT

WEDDING CARS & TRANSPORT CHECKLIST

○ If your wedding has a theme this can often be carried through to the transport in terms of type of vehicle, decoration or simply the colour of the ribbons.

○ Be practical – the rationale for large cars is often as much to do with accommodating the bride's dress as arriving in style, and perhaps an open-topped horse-drawn carriage is not the best choice for a winter wedding.

○ You can co-ordinate colours with ribbons but find out what your car firm will supply or whether you need to supply them with something in advance.

○ Make sure all the parties using the official cars have the phone numbers of the drivers and spare taxi numbers just in case.

○ Make sure the designated person has contact details for the transport provider's office in case of last-minute hitches. However, check beforehand that the office will be open and if not, ask what arrangements they have in place for being contacted on the day in case of emergency.

○ Making sure everyone is in the right place at the right time is crucial. Find out in advance which of your guests will be able to offer lifts and make sure the best man and ushers understand their roles in organising this on the day.

○ Consider if you should provide transport for your guests – particularly if a large family group has come some distance and won't be familiar with the area. Hiring a bus can be a practical option appreciated by guests (who can get in the party spirit together).

○ Make sure the ushers have spare maps to hand out if necessary after the ceremony so guests can find the reception venue.

○ Ask your venue hosts to recommend some taxi companies for guests at the end of the night.

○ Before finalising the times with the transport provider it is a good idea to do a dummy run at a similar time and day as the wedding itself.

○ Find out what time the cars will arrive on the day so you know when to expect them and when it is time to chase if they have not arrived.

- Remember you may need to organise pick-ups for those guests arriving from out of town – friends and family will often help with airport runs but arrange this in advance. See Guests' Travel Arrangements in Guests.

- If you are on a budget consider whether members of the wedding party can travel by taxi or be chauffeured by friends. However, you may get a discount according to the number of cars you book with one provider (and it's less stressful to keep track of one company rather than several).

....

notes

HOW MANY YEARS HAVE YOU BEEN IN BUSINESS?

HOW MANY CARS HAVE YOU AVAILABLE?

MAKE?

MODEL?

COLOUR?

SIZE/CAPACITY?

HOW MANY DRIVERS HAVE YOU AVAILABLE?

ARE YOU AVAILABLE ON _____ (DAY) _____ (TIME)

WHAT IS THE MINIMUM AMOUNT OF TIME FOR RENTING A CAR?

WHAT IS THE COST PER HOUR?

WHAT IS THE PAYMENT POLICY?

WHAT IS THE CANCELLATION POLICY?

DO YOU HAVE LIABILITY INSURANCE?

WILL THE CARS BE DECORATED? IF SO, HOW & WHAT COLOUR?
IF NOT, CAN WE SUPPLY RIBBONS ETC?

CAN YOU PROVIDE A BACK-UP VEHICLE IN CASE OF EMERGENCY?

WILL THE OFFICE BE OPEN ON THE DAY IN CASE OF LAST-MINUTE HITCHES?
IF NOT, CAN YOU GIVE ME A CONTACT NUMBER?

COMPARING

NAME: ADDRESS: WEBSITE: EMAIL: PHONE:	NAME: ADDRESS: WEBSITE: EMAIL: PHONE:

TRANSPORT CONFIRMATION

COMPANY NAME:

ADDRESS:

WEBSITE:

CONTACT NAME:

PHONE:

EMAIL:

EMERGENCY CONTACT NO. ON THE DAY:

DETAILS OF BOOKING:

(NO. OF CARS / MAKE / MODEL / RIBBON COLOUR / NO. OF PEOPLE PER CAR)

BOOKING CONFIRMED: _____ CONTACT: _____

COST:

DEPOSIT: _____ (DUE) _____ (PAID)

BALANCE: _____ (DUE) _____ (PAID)

COMPANY NAME: ....

ADDRESS: ....

....

....

WEBSITE: ....

CONTACT NAME: ....

PHONE: ....

EMAIL: ....

EMERGENCY CONTACT NO. ON THE DAY: ....

....

DETAILS OF BOOKING: ....

(NO. OF CARS / MAKE / MODEL / RIBBON COLOUR / NO. OF PEOPLE PER CAR)

....

....

....

....

....

....

....

....

....

....

....

BOOKING CONFIRMED: _____ CONTACT: _____

COST: ....

DEPOSIT: _____ (DUE) _____ (PAID)

BALANCE: _____ (DUE) _____ (PAID)

TRANSPORT PLANNER

TO THE CEREMONY

NAME	PICK-UP TIME	PICK-UP LOCATION	VEHICLE/DRIVER/ PHONE CONTACT

TO THE RECEPTION

NAME	PICK-UP TIME	PICK-UP LOCATION	VEHICLE/DRIVER/ PHONE CONTACT

AFTER THE RECEPTION

NAME	PICK-UP TIME	PICK-UP LOCATION	VEHICLE/DRIVER/ PHONE CONTACT

LOCAL TAXI NUMBERS FROM CEREMONY/VENUE:

OTHER LOCAL TRANSPORT INFORMATION:

HONEYMOON

HONEYMOON CHECKLIST

Check well in advance what you will need in the way of visas, passport requirements and vaccinations. All of these can take longer to organise than you might expect – particularly if you are jetting off somewhere exotic – so don't leave it until the last minute.

○ Passports (check they are still valid at least 3 months before departure.)

○ Visas

○ Travel vaccinations

○ Holiday money collected

○ Holiday essentials purchased

○ Camera, batteries, memory cards etc

○ Tickets and/or vouchers collected

○ First-night hotel booked

○ Transfer of luggage to hotel/airport organised

○ Transport to hotel/airport booked

○ Transport from airport to home booked

tip
+ If you think you might be spending heavily on your credit card while abroad notify your credit card customer service in advance. This can head off problems when you are away with authorisation due to fraud control.
+ If any bills are due while you are away, make arrangements to pay them before you leave or to delay, with permission, until your return.

HONEYMOON VACCINATIONS

If you are planning a honeymoon in an exotic location check with your doctor or travel agent what vaccinations you will need. Some of them may need to be done weeks in advance and in several phases.

VACCINATIONS NEEDED	WEEKS BEFORE TRAVEL	APPOINTMENT FOR BRIDE	APPOINTMENT FOR GROOM

MEDICINES AND FIRST AID
If you are off to a far-flung destination remember that you may not have easy access to a chemist — even if you are not, do you really want to spend your honeymoon finding somewhere that's open when you are desperate? Think about past holidays or trips and make a list of anything you think you'll need. If you are really going off into the wilds get expert advice about what to take in your first aid kit.

Make a note of your flight details: airline, flight number, departing airport and terminal and check-in time, as well as any specific details such as baggage restrictions. You may also want to make a note of local time when you arrive at your destination and any other flights or journeys you may be making on your honeymoon, with relevant information such as car hire or train travel details. You can make a note of hotel and other contacts overleaf (you can copy these pages if you want family to have your contact details).

HOTEL CONTACTS

HOTEL NAME:

ADDRESS:

WEBSITE:

CONTACT NAME:

PHONE:

EMAIL:

CHECKING IN: CHECKING OUT:

HOTEL NAME:

ADDRESS:

WEBSITE:

CONTACT NAME:

PHONE:

EMAIL:

CHECKING IN: CHECKING OUT:

HOTEL NAME:

ADDRESS:

WEBSITE:

CONTACT NAME:

PHONE:

EMAIL:

CHECKING IN: CHECKING OUT:

HOTEL CONTACTS

HOTEL NAME:

ADDRESS:

WEBSITE:

CONTACT NAME:

PHONE:

EMAIL:

CHECKING IN: CHECKING OUT:

HOTEL NAME:

ADDRESS:

WEBSITE:

CONTACT NAME:

PHONE:

EMAIL:

CHECKING IN: CHECKING OUT:

HOTEL NAME:

ADDRESS:

WEBSITE:

CONTACT NAME:

PHONE:

EMAIL:

CHECKING IN: CHECKING OUT:

TRAVEL INSURANCE DETAILS

Check your policy to make sure you are covered for any extra activities you may be doing such as winter sports, diving or any extreme activities.

POLICY FOR:

POLICY NUMBER:

VALID FROM: VALID UNTIL:

COST:

COMPANY NAME:

ADDRESS:

PHONE:

EMAIL:

CLAIMS TELEPHONE HOTLINE:

POLICY FOR:

POLICY NUMBER:

VALID FROM: VALID UNTIL:

COST:

COMPANY NAME:

ADDRESS:

PHONE:

EMAIL:

CLAIMS TELEPHONE HOTLINE:

Brimming with creative inspiration, how-to projects and useful
information to enrich your everyday life, Quarto Knows is a
favourite destination for those pursuing their interests and passions.
Visit our site and dig deeper with our books into your area of interest:
Quarto Creates, Quarto Cooks, Quarto Homes, Quarto Lives,
Quarto Drives, Quarto Explores, Quarto Gifts, or Quarto Kids.

Wedding Planner
© 2017 Quarto Publishing plc.
Confetti image © Anna Hoychuk/Shutterstock, *Round ink stain* © Saibarakova Ilona/Shutterstock,
Banner © PinkPueblo/Shutterstock

First published in 2017 by Frances Lincoln, an imprint of The Quarto Group,
The Old Brewery, 6 Blundell Street, London N7 9BH, United Kingdom
www.QuartoKnows.com

A catalogue record for this book is available from the British Library

ISBN 978-0-7112-3913-5

Design by Sarah Allberrey

Printed and bound in China

9 8 7 6 5 4